I0815340

Zodiac Signs

An Imprint of Pop!
popbooksonline.com

AQUARIUS

by Elizabeth Andrews

WELCOME TO DiscoverRoo!

This book is filled with videos, puzzles, games, and more! Scan the QR codes* while you read, or visit the website below to make this book pop.

popbooksonline.com/aqua

abdobooks.com

Published by Pop!, a division of ABDO, PO Box 398166, Minneapolis, Minnesota 55439.

Printed in the United States of America, North Mankato, Minnesota.

042025
082025

THIS BOOK CONTAINS RECYCLED MATERIALS

Cover Photo: Splendoura Prints; Shutterstock Images
Interior Photos: Getty Images; Shutterstock Images
Editor: Tyler Gieseke
Series Designer: Laura Graphenteen

Library of Congress Control Number: 2024948383

Publisher's Cataloging-in-Publication Data

Names: Andrews, Elizabeth, author.
Title: Aquarius / by Elizabeth Andrews
Description: Minneapolis, Minnesota : Pop!, 2026 | Series: Zodiac signs | Includes online resources and index
Identifiers: ISBN 9781098247867 (lib. bdg.) | ISBN 9781098248406 (ebook)
Subjects: LCSH: Aquarius (Astrology)--Juvenile literature. | Water bearer (Astrology)--Juvenile literature. | Zodiac--Juvenile literature. | Astrology--Juvenile literature. | Astrology--Charts, diagrams, etc.--Juvenile literature.
Classification: DDC 133.52--dc23

*Scanning QR codes requires a web-enabled smart device with a QR code reader app and a camera.

TABLE OF CONTENTS

CHAPTER 1

MEET THE AQUARIUS!

Aquarius is the eleventh sign of the zodiac. Aquarians are born between January 20 and February 18. When people ask for your "star sign," they are likely asking for your sun sign. This is the zodiac sign the sun appeared in at your birth.

Orchid

January 20–February 18

AQUARIUS

constellation

masculine

amethyst

fixed

1

numbers

7

WED

symbol

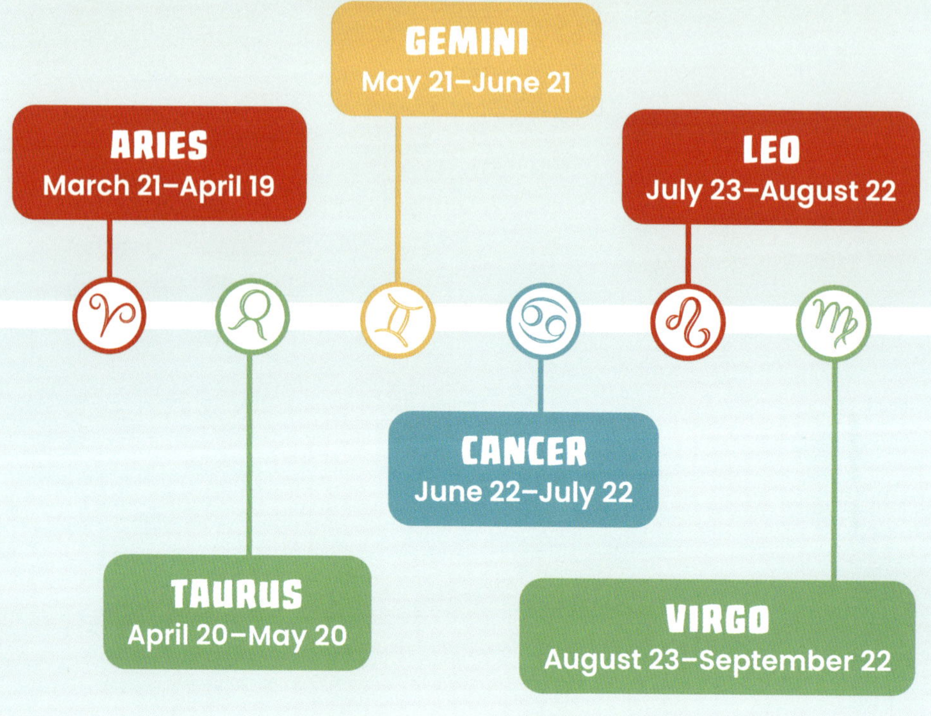

Three features help describe zodiac signs. Signs can be masculine or feminine. Each zodiac sign is given a mode. The three modes are cardinal, fixed, and mutable. Each zodiac is also

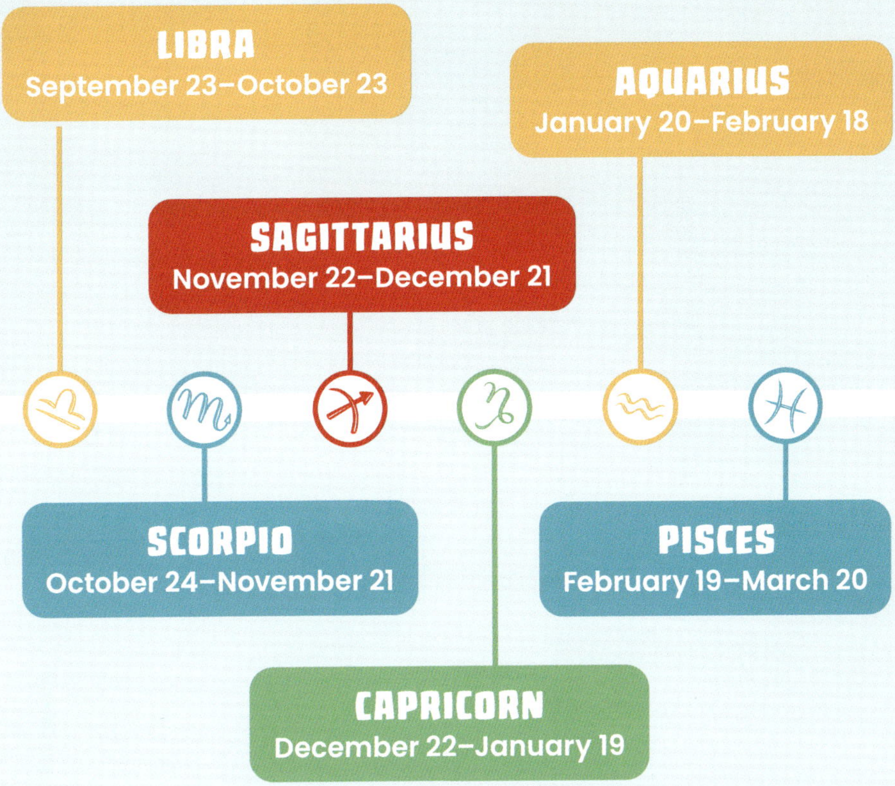
LIBRA
September 23–October 23
AQUARIUS
January 20–February 18
SAGITTARIUS
November 22–December 21
SCORPIO
October 24–November 21
PISCES
February 19–March 20
CAPRICORN
December 22–January 19

a fire, air, earth, or water sign. No zodiac sign shares the same three features.

DID YOU KNOW?

Aquarians get along best with fire and other air signs.

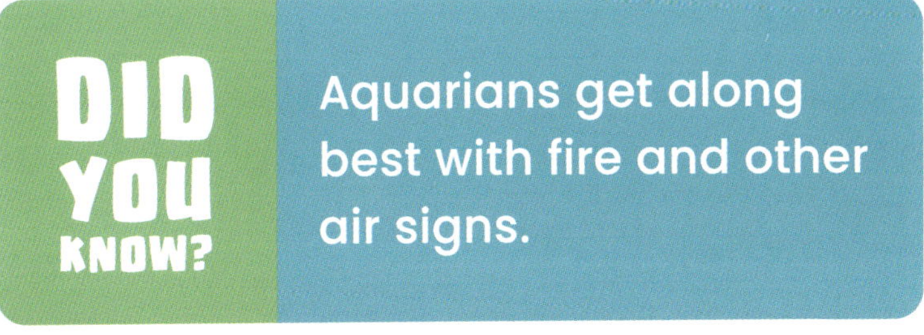

Air signs are good at keeping their minds clear from worries. Taking walks in fresh air help them with this.

Aquarius is a masculine, fixed, air sign. People with masculine signs are reasonable and action focused. They usually say exactly what they mean. They are outgoing and strong.

Modes determine how signs interact with the outside world. Fixed signs are very grounded. This means that they are emotionally stable and clear thinkers. They don't like change. Air signs are smart and talkative. They are often curious and quirky.

Fixed signs are reliable. This means they can be trusted.

Aquarius is **represented** by the water bearer. The water being poured **symbolizes** the truth Aquarians give freely to the world. Some ancient people connected Aquarius to their water god who flooded their lands every year to help grow food. Ancient Greeks connected the Aquarius **constellation** to Ganymede. He was a young boy taken by Zeus to serve the gods.

The Aquarius constellation can be seen in the fall in the Northern Hemisphere and spring in the Southern Hemisphere.

Zeus turned into an eagle to bring Ganymede to Mount Olympus.

CHAPTER 2

HISTORY OF ASTROLOGY

Humans have searched for life's **spiritual** meaning since the beginning of time. They often looked to the stars for this. Astrology is the practice of reading the movements of planets and other **celestial** bodies and connecting them to life on Earth.

LEARN MORE HERE!

Some ancient people used the zodiac signs to predict future events.

Babylonians invented the zodiac in Mesopotamia over 5,000 years ago. Mesopotamia was the first known civilization. Babylon was one of the region's largest cities.

Ptolemy was an Egyptian man who studied the stars.

Earth and our solar system are in the Milky Way galaxy.

The zodiac is a belt of space around Earth that has 12 well-known **constellations**. Ancient people noticed that the sun seemed to move in front of these constellations throughout a year. The sun spends about a month in each constellation.

The constellations in the zodiac belt are Aries, Taurus, Gemini, Cancer, Leo, Virgo, Libra, Scorpius, Sagittarius, Capricornus, Aquarius, and Pisces. Together they make up the 12 zodiac signs. They are all **represented** by different **symbols**.

Islamic astrologers created new ways to map and measure stars.

THE ZODIAC WHEEL

DID YOU KNOW?

Most zodiac symbols are animals. The ancient Greeks called the belt of space *zodiakos kyklos,* or "circle of animals."

CHAPTER 3

AN ORIGINAL

Aquarius is ruled by the planet Uranus. Uranus is the planet of the unexpected. It is the planet of change for the better. Aquarians are smart, independent people. They have big dreams and ideas. They want the world to be a better place for everyone.

EXPLORE LINKS HERE!

Harry Styles is an Aquarius. He often performs in cool, unexpected outfits.

Aquarians find special ways to share their ideas.

No one is like an Aquarius. Aquarians do not need to count on other people to help them or give them ideas. They march to the beat of their own drum. Aquarians believe nothing is better than having the freedom to be themselves. They do not follow trends.

Aquarius is an air sign. Air signs are often smart and good **communicators**. Aquarians are always asking *"Why?"* They are curious about the world around them and want to discover new things. Aquarians are rational people. They don't let emotions get in the way of learning the truth.

Aquarians enjoy exploring nature. It is an adventure for them!

Aquarians often do well in science and art classes. They like experimenting.

Aquarians connect themselves to their ideas. Their sign is the water bearer. For Aquarians, their ideas are what they pour out. They see themselves as truth tellers and freely share their opinions and observations. They are proud of what their minds can do. Aquarians express their ideas creatively.

DID YOU KNOW?

Sometimes Aquarians don't follow the rules. They think they know better!

CHAPTER 4

WORLD CHANGER

Aquarians like people. They are truly themselves with anyone they meet. Aquarians like to watch and learn from the people they surround themselves with. They can get along well with all kinds of personalities.

COMPLETE AN ACTIVITY HERE!

Amethyst is a calming stone.

Some Aquarians care very deeply about protecting the planet.

Friends of Aquarians think they are funny and curious. Aquarians' smarts give them a good sense of humor. They can make people laugh with just a few words. Aquarians are not judgmental and want the people they love to be happy. They are true friends. However, Aquarians sometimes keep their friends at arm's length to stay independent.

DID YOU KNOW?

While Aquarians have big ideas, they don't like all the hard work it takes to put them into action.

Susan B. Anthony was an Aquarian. She fought for the rights of women and enslaved people in the 1800s.

Aquarius is the sign of revolution. A revolution is a sudden or complete change. Aquarians want the world to be a better place for everyone. They are often concerned with world issues, such as war, hunger, and **climate**.

Bob Marley was a Jamaican musician who stood for peace and social justice. He was an Aquarius.

Aquarians like to work with groups who have the same dreams of change. They would do well in jobs that center on **social justice** or politics. These jobs can give Aquarians the opportunity to change the world with their big ideas.

Today, astrology can answer questions about an individual. People use astrology to understand who they are and why they might do what they do. It can also help them understand other people in their life. A zodiac sign can point out personal skills, possibilities, and **internal motivations**.

WHAT IS A BIRTH CHART?

Each person's birth chart contains all the planets in our solar system, the moon, and the sun. The location of where each **celestial** body was based on the exact time and location of a person's birth can be marked on a birth chart. A birth chart can explain even more about a person than what only a sun sign can. The placement of each planet affects the drive of a person. This reveals personal motivations. Astrology experts can read birth charts.

MAKING CONNECTIONS

TEXT-TO-SELF

Are you an Aquarius? If so, do you think the sign matches your personality? If not, what do you have in common with Aquarians?

TEXT-TO-TEXT

Have you read any books about the other zodiac signs? How were those signs similar to and different from Aquarians?

TEXT-TO-WORLD

With the help of an adult, look up famous Aquarians. Pick one person and write a few sentences about ways that person shows Aquarian qualities.

GLOSSARY

celestial — having to do with the sky or outer space.

climate — the typical weather of a place or area over time.

communicator — a person who shares information and knowledge with others.

constellation — a group of stars that forms a pattern.

internal — of, relating to, or being on the inside.

motivation — something that makes one want to do something.

represent — to stand for or be a sign of.

social justice — the belief that all people should have equal rights and opportunities.

spiritual — having to do with people's beliefs in things such as the soul, nature, and what happens after death.

symbol — an object or picture that represents something else.

INDEX